POP QUARTETS for all

Playable on ANY FOUR INSTRUMENTS
or any number of instruments in ensemble

Arranged by Michael Story

CONTENTS

Instrumentation

30709	Piano/Conductor/Oboe		30715	Horn in F
30710	Flute/Piccolo		30716	Trombone/Baritone/Bassoon/Tuba
30711	B♭ Clarinet/Bass Clarinet		30717	Violin
30712	Alto Saxophone (E♭ Saxes and E♭ Clarinets)		30718	Viola
30713	Tenor Saxophone		30719	Cello/String Bass
30714	B♭ Trumpet/Baritone T.C.		30720	Percussion

Alfred Music
P.O. Box 10003
Van Nuys, CA 91410-0003
alfred.com

ISBN-10: 0-7390-5459-7
ISBN-13: 978-0-7390-5459-8

SUMMERTIME
(From PORGY AND BESS®)

By GEORGE GERSHWIN,
DU BOSE and DOROTHY HEYWARD,
and IRA GERSHWIN
Arranged by MICHAEL STORY

VIOLA

CELEBRATION

Words and Music by
RONALD BELL, CLAYDES SMITH, GEORGE BROWN,
JAMES TAYLOR, ROBERT MICKENS, EARL TOON,
DENNIS THOMAS, ROBERT BELL, and EUMIR DEODATO
Arranged by MICHAEL STORY

30718

30718

WE ARE FAMILY

Words and Music by
BERNARD EDWARDS and NILE RODGERS
Arranged by MICHAEL STORY

BATMAN THEME

Words and Music by NEAL HEFTI
Arranged by MICHAEL STORY

IMPERIAL MARCH
(Darth Vader's Theme)

By JOHN WILLIAMS
Arranged by MICHAEL STORY

30718

THEME FROM "ICE CASTLES"
(Through the Eyes of Love)

Music by MARVIN HAMLISCH
Lyrics by CAROLE BAYER SAGER
Arranged by MICHAEL STORY

JUMP

Words and Music by
EDWARD VAN HALEN, ALEX VAN HALEN,
MICHAEL ANTHONY, and DAVID LEE ROTH
Arranged by MICHAEL STORY

Bright rock

IT DON'T MEAN A THING
(If It Ain't Got That Swing)

Words by IRVING MILLS
Music by DUKE ELLINGTON
Arranged by MICHAEL STORY

JAMES BOND THEME

Music by MONTY NORMAN
Arranged by MICHAEL STORY

SMOOTH

Words and Music by
ITAAL SHUR and **ROB THOMAS**
Arranged by MICHAEL STORY

GONNA FLY NOW
(Theme From "ROCKY")

By BILL CONTI, AYN ROBBINS,
and CAROL CONNORS
Arranged by MICHAEL STORY

PETER GUNN
(From "Peter Gunn")

By HENRY MANCINI
Arranged by MICHAEL STORY

Driving